Date Due			

ASTRONAUTS WORK IN SPACE

Design and Art Direction
Lindaanne Donohoe Design

●▲●▼●▲●●▲●▼●▲●

Picture Acknowledgments

Photographs courtesy of NASA,
the National Aeronautics and Space Administration

●▲●▼●▲●●▲●▼●▲●

Library of Congress Cataloging-in-Publication Data

Greene, Carol.

Astronauts work in space/by Carol Greene.
p.   cm.
Summary: Photographs and simple text describe some of the
jobs that astronauts do aboard a space shuttle and
what they do to prepare on the ground.
ISBN 1-56766-406-7
1. Astronautics — Juvenile literature.
[1. Astronauts. 2. Astronautics.] I. Title.

TL793.G7623   1997   97-3657
629.45'0092—dc21   CIP
                                                    AC

ASTRONAUTS
WORK IN SPACE

By Carol Greene

THE CHILD'S WORLD®

*L*IFT-OFF!   WOW!

The shuttle zooms into the sky.

It is on its way into space.

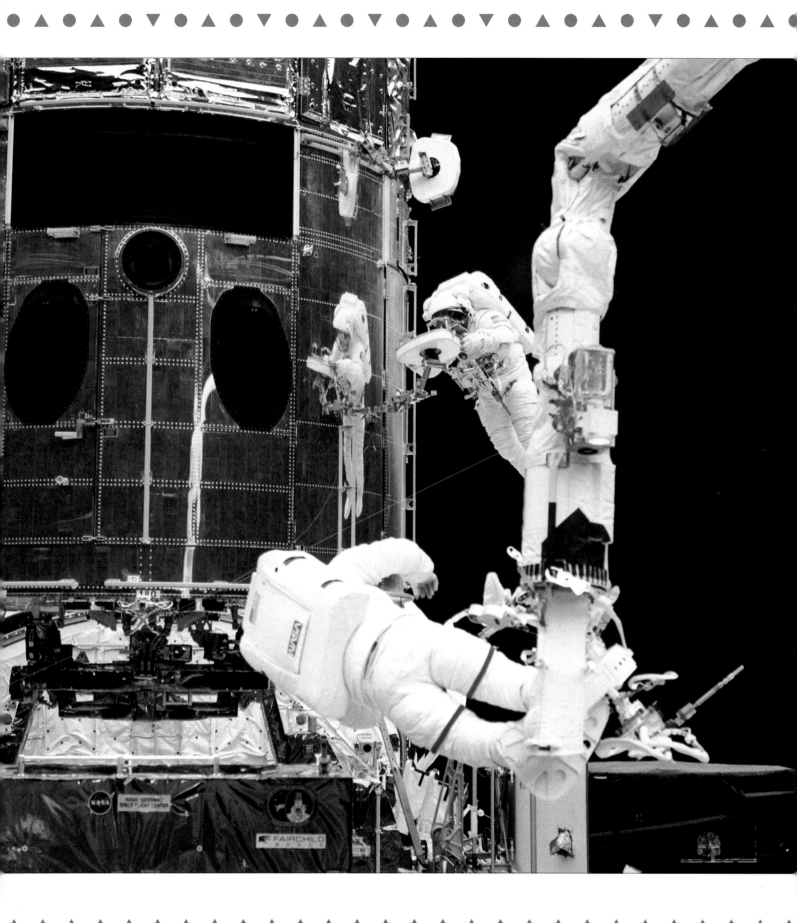

A team of astronauts work

aboard the space shuttle.

Each astronaut has a special job.

Pilot astronauts fly the shuttle.

They handle the controls.

TAP! TAP! TAP!

Pilot astronauts are in charge

of the shuttle.

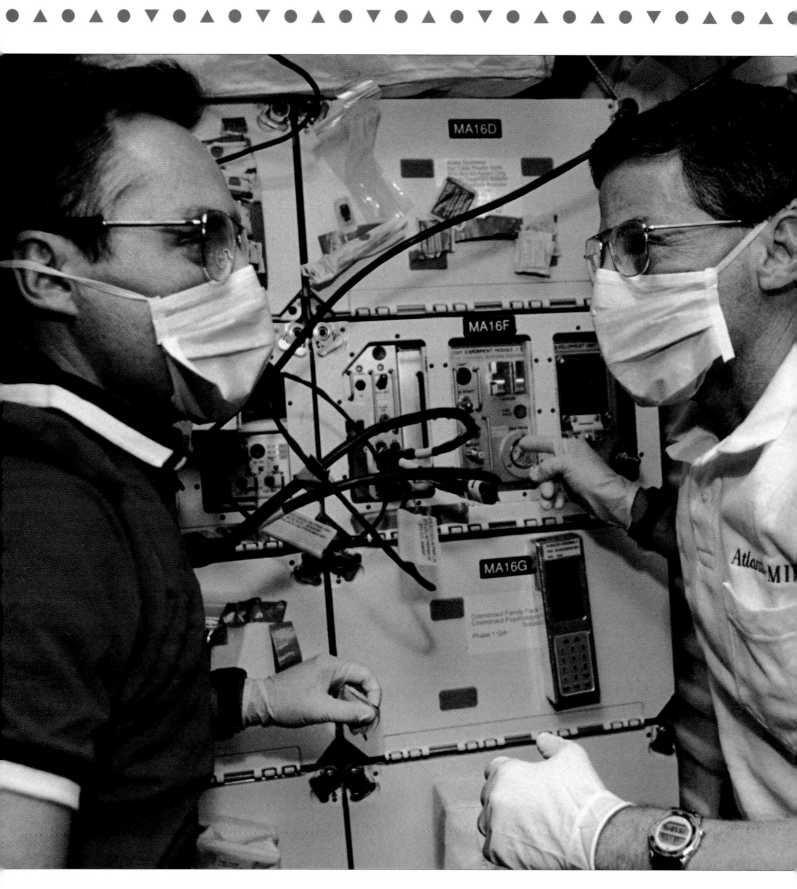

Other astronauts take care of

the shuttle and all its parts.

CLICK! CLICK!

This astronaut is walking in space.

WHEEE!

It feels like floating on water—

but is even better.

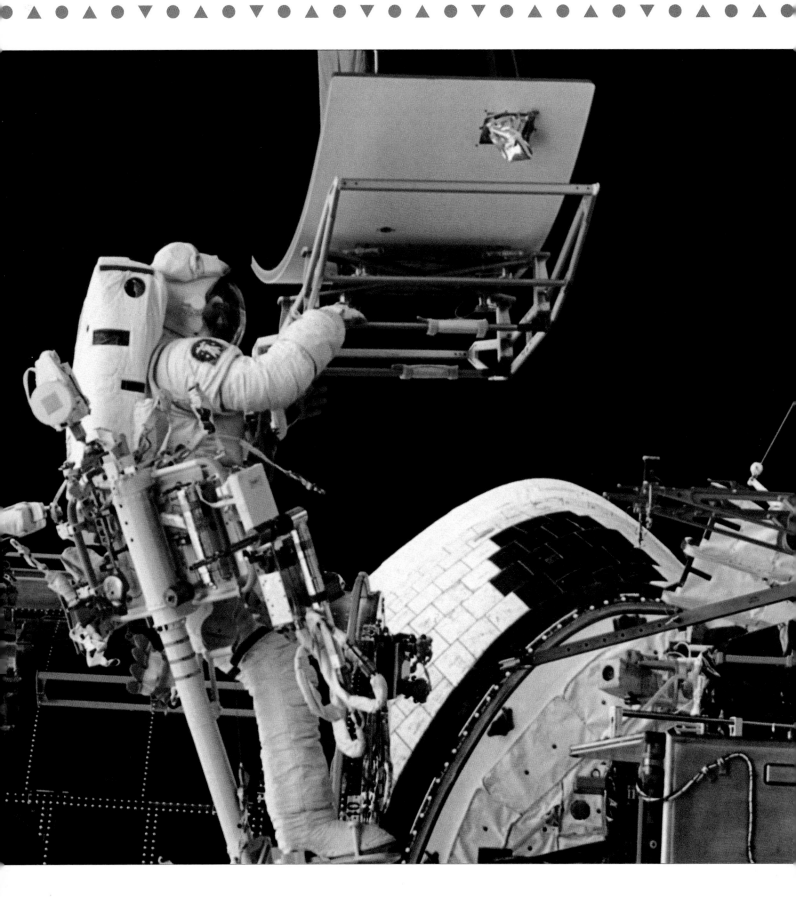

This space shuttle carries a big machine.

It belongs to a science company.

This astronaut does experiments

with the machine.

ZZZZZZZ! POP!

Astronauts on the ground talk

to astronauts in the shuttle.

YAKITY! YAK!

They help the trip run smoothly.

All astronauts learn their jobs

at The Johnson Space Center

in Houston, Texas.

This is a big place with many workers.

All space trips begin here.

NASA, the National Aeronautics

and Space Administration,

runs the Space Center.

It is part of the United States

government. NASA picks and trains

the people who will be astronauts.

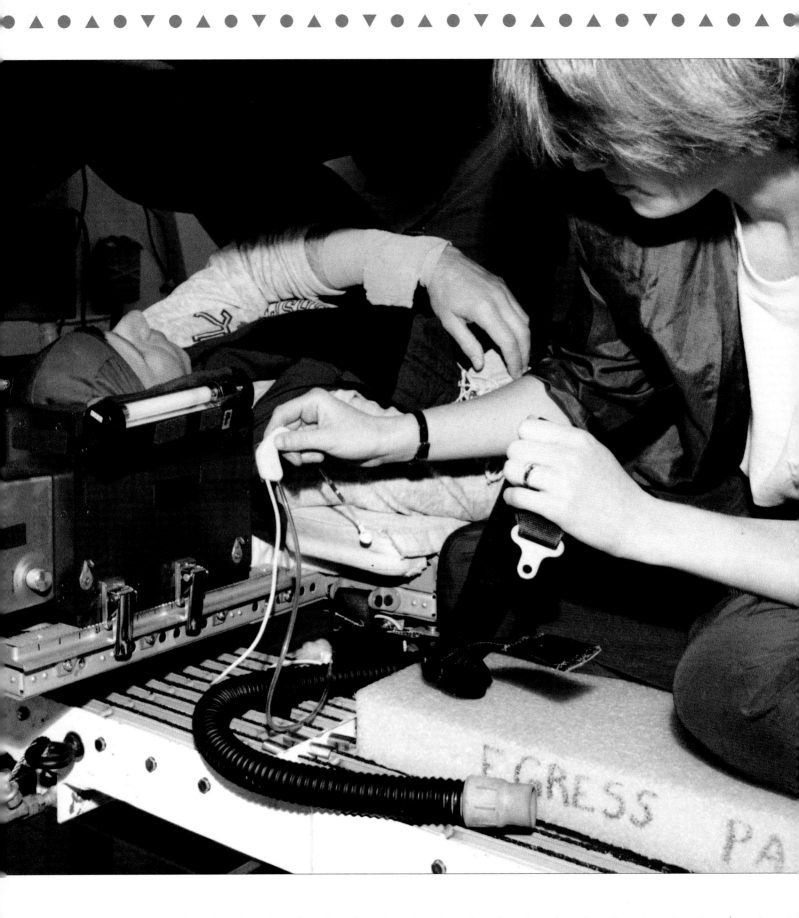

These people train for a year at
the Space Center. Astronauts learn
how the space shuttle works.
They do many kinds of experiments.

Astronauts practice in a

full-size model of the shuttle.

TAP! TAP!

They spend a lot of time

pretending to fly in space.

Astronauts practice a lot.

They try to solve problems they might

have in space. What would they

do if this computer stopped working?

What would they do if an engine

stopped working?

Astronauts work hard in the classroom.

They learn to do many things.

They must be healthy and fit.

When they are ready they must

wait for the shuttle flight that

is right for them.

Here comes the space shuttle.

WHOOSH!

Welcome aboard, astronauts!

Questions and Answers

What do astronauts do?

Astronauts work in space. Some are pilots who fly the shuttle. Others take care of the spacecraft and do science experiments. Astronauts work on the ground jobs too. They help astronauts in space. They also help plan space flights and new spacecrafts.

How do people learn to be astronauts?

All astronauts must go to college for four years. They study engineering, science, or math. Most go on to graduate school to learn even more. Then they must pass NASA's physical tests. They study for a year at the Johnson Space Center. Most pilot astronauts are test pilots for the United States armed forces.

What kind of people are astronauts?

Astronauts must be strong and smart. They should be very good at science. Astronauts must get along well with other people. They spend a lot of time working with a team. And they must not mind being in small spaces.

How much money do astronauts make?

Pilot astronauts are paid according to their military rank. Astronauts who are not in the military make about $55,000 dollars a year.

GLOSSARY

astronaut—person trained to work in space

computer—a special machine that can hold information and can quickly give answers

controls—a set of instruments used to start, steer, and stop a machine

engine—the piece of equipment that is built to give power to a machine, such as an airplane

experiments—tests done to find out how something works or to see if what you think is true is always true

flight—the motion of an object usually an airplane, through the air

lift-off—take off

model—a copy of a larger object

NASA—the National Aeronautics and Space Administration—the name of the part of the government that is in charge of the space program for the United States of America

pilot—person who knows how to fly a plane or a space shuttle

practice—to do something again and again in order to do the same thing quickly and correctly

problems—difficulties; troubles

shuttle—the craft build to allow astronauts to fly into and return from space

space—the huge place where the planets, sun, stars, and other heavenly objects are found

spacecraft—name for objects built to fly into space safely

team—group of people who work together for the same goal

CAROL GREENE has written over 200 books for children. She also likes to read books, make teddy bears, work in her garden, and sing. Ms. Greene lives in Webster Groves, Missouri.